Illustrated Dictionary
of
Computer Terms

Davinder Singh Minhas

RISING SUN

RISING SUN
an imprint of
New Dawn Press

NEW DAWN PRESS GROUP
New Dawn Press, Inc., 244 South Randall Rd # 90, Elgin, IL 60123
e-mail: sales@newdawnpress.com
New Dawn Press, 2 Tintern Close, Slough, Berkshire, SL1-2TB, UK
e-mail: ndpuk@newdawnpress.com
          sterlingdis@yahoo.co.uk

New Dawn Press (An Imprint of Sterling Publishers (P) Ltd.)

A-59, Okhla Industrial Area, Phase-II, New Delhi-110020
e-mail: sterlingpublishers@touchtelindia.net
          Ghai@nde.vsnl.net.in

© 2005, New Dawn Press

Printed at Sterling Publishers Pvt. Ltd., New Delhi

Introduction

With rapid developments in computing technology, computing terminology has also expanded. Recent advances in all aspects of computing - software, hardware, approaches to programming, networking, computer applications and operating systems, have led to the coining of new terms and expansion in meaning of existing terms. In order to keep the user up-to-date with latest developments in technology, these new terms have been incorporated in the *Illustrated Dictionary of Computer Terms*. It offers a comprehensive coverage of the various terms used in computing.

The terms described range from the basic functions and concepts related to computers, to the common as well as latest physical components and equipments of a computer. The entries are alphabetically listed with clear and concise explanations and illustrations. The entire book has been specially designed in a reader-friendly format, so that users are able to access the information they seek without difficulty.

As a student's handbook and for the general reader, this dictionary is an excellent guide to the many computing terms that are now so much a part of our daily lives.

Adapter: It is an interface card that can be installed in a personal computer to allow it to use additional peripheral devices or hardware. A video adapter, for example, allows a computer to connect to a monitor.

Accessories: These are handy little tools which an operating system like Windows is equipped with. Some handy tools that you can use are calculator and notepad.

Alignment: The manner in which you make your text fit between the right and left margins of a page is called alignment. With this feature, you can right-align, center, left-align or fully align your text. The last style of alignment is also known as justification.

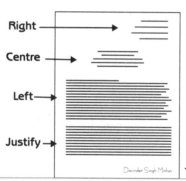

Active Window: A window is in the form of a rectangle on your screen. The active window refers to the window that you are currently working on.

Alt Key: It is a keyboard key that is mostly pressed with another letter or digit key to give a command to the computer. For example, in Windows, holding down the Alt key and pressing F displays the File menu.

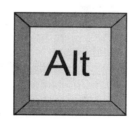

Anti-Glare Screen: It is a transparent screen which fits over the front of a monitor to reduce eye strain. It decreases the amount of light reflected by the computer screen.

Application Software: You can use application software to write letters, analyze numbers, draw pictures, and even play games and also accomplish specific tasks. Some popular softwares are: MS-Word, MS-Excel, and MS-Access.

Arrow Keys: These are the four keys placed on the keyboard labeled with arrows pointing up, down, left, and right. They are used to move the cursor vertically or horizontally on the display screen.

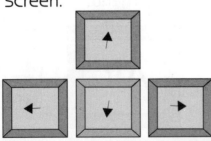

AT: Abbreviation of **A**dvanced **T**echnology. IBM's first 286-based PC was introduced in 1984. It was the most advanced machine in the PC line and featured a new keyboard, 1.2 MB floppy and 16-bit data bus.

Attachment: Any type of file can be attached to an e-mail message so that they travel to their destination together. For e.g., text file, a database, spreadsheet, graphics or program files.

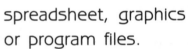

Automatic Carriage Return: This feature automatically wraps the text to the next line once you reach the end of a line while typing. You do not need to press Enter key to begin a new line of the text when one line is full as the cursor automatically moves on to the next line.

When you use a Microsoft word to type a letter, the text automatically wraps to the next line as you type.

Bad Sector: A damaged portion of your floppy or hard disk that will no longer store information reliably. If your hard disk has a bad sector, you can run special software to fix the bad sector.

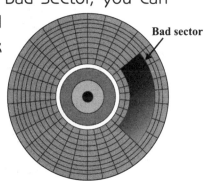

Bad sector

Backspace key: A key that moves the cursor one space to the left and deletes whatever character is there. Backspace is the last key in the row of number keys. It has a backward arrow marked on it.

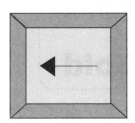

Batch Processing: A group of documents or files processed all at one time. For example, you can collect all your reports and take a printout of them as one batch.

Bad Disk: A disk which is no longer good for storing information. In case you have a bad disk, it is always better to copy your work to another disk and get rid of the floppy.

Bay: The shelf where your hard drive, CD-ROM drive, and floppy drive are placed in your computer case.

Bay

Bezier Curves: Bezier curves are typically reshaped by moving the handles that appear off of the curve.

Bit: The smallest unit of memory is called bit. It is also known as **binary digit.** In the binary number system, the digits 0 and 1 are also called bits and represent on and off position respectively.

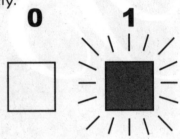

Binary file: It is a file containing numeric data or program instructions in a language that only computers can understand.

0101001

Bold: It means to show characters with thicker and darker strokes. One can highlight important information by typing the text in bold letters.

Normal

Bold

BIOS (Basic Input/Output System): It is a set of instructions that guides the computer how to function or transfer data and instructions. For example, disk drives, visual display unit and keyboard are controlled by BIOS.

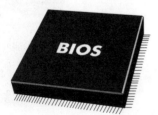

Byte: A byte is a unit of information stored in a computer, equal to eight bits. Every character or symbol entered into the computer takes up one byte of memory. Each byte is stored in a cell at a particular address.

The Byte

| 0 | 1 | 0 | 0 | 1 | 1 | 0 | 1 |

A byte is 8 binary digits, or cells.

Capacity: The number of bytes (characters) a storage medium can hold. For example, a 40-megabyte hard disk has the capacity to hold forty million bytes of data.

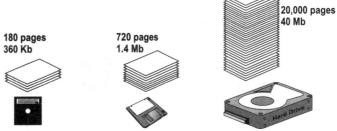

180 pages
360 Kb

720 pages
1.4 Mb

20,000 pages
40 Mb

Cache: The cache is a section of RAM that stores copies of data that is often needed while a program is running. Whenever the computer needs data, it first looks for it in the cache. The cache can supply data thousands of times faster than the hard drive.

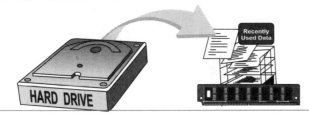

Caps Lock Key: It is a key that changes the alphabetic characters on the keyboard to uppercase. The Caps Lock key does not affect numbers, punctuation marks, or other symbols.

Calculator: It is a program or a part of an operating system that enables the user to perform arithmetic calculations. The calculator is operated with the keyboard or with a mouse.

Cascade: It is a manner of arranging all the open windows on your screen in a way that each window overlaps each other, showing only the title bar to show their names.

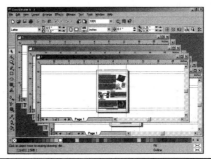

Case: A computer case contains the major components of a computer system. There are two types of cases, namely desktop case and tower case. A desktop case usually sits on a desk, under a monitor. A tower case stands vertical on the table.

Desktop — Tower case

Click: Click means to press and release a button on your mouse. You can click on the mouse button to give a command to the computer.

>Click

CD-ROM: Stands for **C**ompact **D**isc-**R**ead-**O**nly **M**emory and it looks just like a music CD. A single CD-ROM disc can store up to 700 Mb of data. The large storage capacity of a CD-ROM disc makes installing new programs on your computer easy.

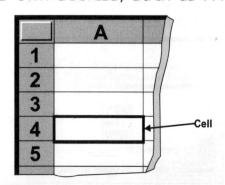

PROGRAMS
disc
CD-ROM

Computer: A computer is a general purpose machine which can perform many day-to-day works. The equipments attached to a computer are called hardware. The instructions or programs used to operate the computer are called software.

Cell: A cell is a basic unit in a spreadsheet program in which you can enter data. Each cell in a spreadsheet has its own address, such as A4.

	A
1	
2	
3	
4	←Cell
5	

Control Key: This key is pressed with a letter or digit key to command the computer; for example, holding down the **control key** and pressing **B** will make your character bold in most of the word processors.

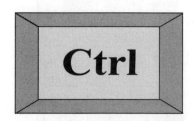

Ctrl

Device: A device is a hardware component or machine that is attached to your computer. Printers, modems, CD-ROM drives, keyboards and mouse are some of the devices.

Delete Key: Abbreviated as Del. Pressing this key on the keyboard erases the character on the right of cursor.

Dialog Box: It is a rectangular box that appears on the screen to display options. Some dialog box ask users to make a choice. Once the choice is made the computer carries out the command.

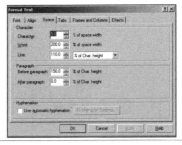

Desktop: A desktop is a display on a computer screen. The desktop display may show icons, menus, windows and text within the windows.

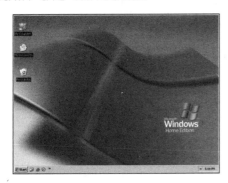

Digital Camera: It is a device which lets you take photographs that you can use on your computer. You can transfer photos from a digital camera to a computer. This lets you use the photos in documents on the World Wide Web or in e-mail messages.

Dingbats: These are special characters like stars, hands, arrows, and geometric shapes that you can use to decorate a document.

Domain Name: It is the location of the person's account on the Internet. An e-mail address consists of two parts (User name and Domain name) separated by the @ symbol.

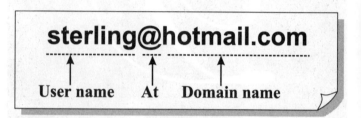

Directory: It is also called a folder. Your computer stores programs and data in drives. A drive contains directories to organize your information. A directory usually contains related information. For example, the 'game' directory contains all your favorite games.

DOS (**D**isk **O**perating **S**ystem): It is a single-user operating system launched by Microsoft for the personal computer (PC) and was the first operating system for the PC.

Diskette: It is mostly used by personal computer users to save their data. Diskettes are transferable from one computer to another. 5¼-inch diskette and 3½-inch diskette are two sizes of diskette.

Dot-matrix Printer: A noisy, inexpensive printer that produces characters made up of dots using a wire-pin print head.

E-mail Address: The address to which an e-mail message is sent is called an e-mail address. An e-mail address consists of two parts (User name and Domain name) separated by the @ symbol. The symbol @ means at.

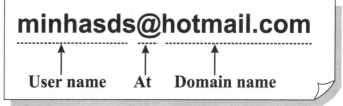

minhasds@hotmail.com

User name   At   Domain name

E-commerce: Also called e-business and e-tailing, it typically implies purchasing products via the Web and doing business online.

E-mail Program: An e-mail program lets you send, receive and manage your e-mail messages. The most popular e-mail programs are Microsoft Outlook, Yahoo Messenger and Eudora.

E-mail: Short for **e**lectronic **m**ail, it implies the exchange of text messages and computer files over a communications network, or the Internet, usually between computers.

Emoticons: It is an expression of emotion typed into a message using standard keyboard characters. These characters look like human faces when you turn them sideways. For eg, like this **:-)** means **smile**.

Enhanced Keyboard: An enhanced keyboard contains 101-105 keys, a row of function keys at the top rather than on the left side and an extra set of cursor control keys between the main typing keys and the numeric keypad.

Enter Key: This key is pressed to use at the end of a line to instruct the computer wrap the text to the next line. In word processing programs like MS-Word, the Enter key is used at the end of a paragraph. Enter key is also called the return key.

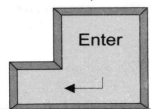

Ethernet: It is one of the most popular and inexpensive way an information can travel through the network. Ethernet can send information through a network at a speed of 10 megabits per second (Mbps).

Expansion Card: An expansion card is a circuit board that lets you add new features to a computer.

Expansion Slot: An expansion slot is a socket where you plug in an expansion card. The number of expansion slots your computer has affects the number of features you can add to your computer.

Expansion card

Expansion slot

External Modem: An external modem is a small box that uses a cable to connect to the back of a computer. It is generally connected to the serial port or USB (**U**niversal **S**erial **B**us) port. An external modem can be moved easily and set up on another computer.

File: Almost all information stored in a computer is saved in a file. There are many different types of files: text files, program files, audio-video files, etc. Different types of files store different types of information. All data that has a name is called the file name. A file extension is an addition to a file name. It usually contains three characters that follow a full stop.

Fax Machine: It is a device that sends and receives printed pages over telephone lines by converting them into electrical signals. A fax machine is also known as facsimile machine.

Firewall: It is a security system that is used to protect an organization network against external threats, such as hackers from another network, such as the Internet.

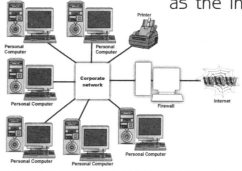

Fax Modem: It is a device that enables you to transmit and receive electronic documents as faxes when connected to a personal computer. A fax modem is like a regular modem except that it is designed to transmit documents to a fax machine or to another fax modem.

Flatbed Scanner: It is used to scan single sheets of paper and pages from a book. A flatbed scanner creates clearer images than a hand-held scanner. The function of a flatbed scanner is the same as that of a photocopier.

Floppy Disks: It is mostly used by personal computer users to save their data. Floppy disk is transferable from one computer to another. 5¼-inch diskette and 3½-inch diskette are two sizes of floppy disks.

Floppy Disk Drive (FDD): A floppy drive stores and retrieves information on floppy disks. Most computers have a floppy drive, called drive A.

Flowchart: It is a diagram or map showing the steps taken to reach a certain result. Flowcharts contain boxes of different shapes connected to each other by lines.

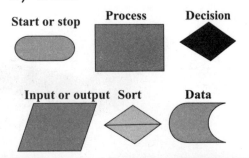

Font: It is the particular size and style of a set of letters that are used in typing. Arial, Benguiat BK BT are some examples of different fonts.

AllegroBT

Times New Roman

Arial

Format Disk: To prepare a disk so that it can store information, you need to format it. It divides the storage area into tracks and sectors on it which will hold data.

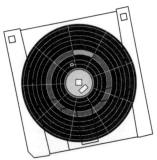

Function Keys: Function keys are situated above the number keys on the keyboard. They are marked F1 to F12. Each of these keys is used for performing a special function/job.

Gradient: It is a smooth blending of shades from light to dark or from one color to another.

Gigabyte: One gigabyte is equal to 1,073,741,824 characters. This is approximately equal to a bunch of books in a book stand. Gigabyte is often abbreviated as GB.

Graphics: It is the display of pictorial information by computers.

Grabber Hand: It is a screen tool that is shaped like a hand and is used to move objects within a window. It is also known as hand tool.

Graphics Card: It is a high-performance display adapter that can be fitted into a expansion slot at the back of the computer and it gives the computer the functions it needs to run the graphics programs.

Hand-Held Scanner: A hand-held scanner usually has a scanning width of approximately four inches and is useful for copying small images such as signature, logos and small photographs.

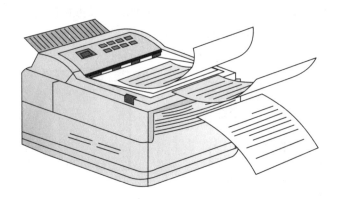

Hackers: Hackers are programmers who attempt to breach the security of a computer system by access from a remote point, especially by guessing or otherwise obtaining a password.

Hard Copy: A hard copy is the printed information of any data that is stored in the computer.

Hand-held Computer: A hand-held computer is a portable computer that is small enough to fit in your hand.

Hard Drive: It is the storage device that a computer uses to store information. The hard disk inside the system unit is sometimes called **fixed disk**. A hard drive with a capacity of 20 to 80 GB is most suitable for home and business users.

Hardware: The electronic components of a computer that can be seen or touched are collectively known as hardware.

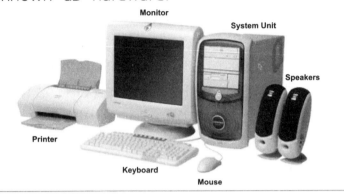

Home Key: It is the keyboard key that moves the cursor or insertion point to the beginning of the line, screen, or file.

Home Network: It is a network that connects multiple computers in a home or office.

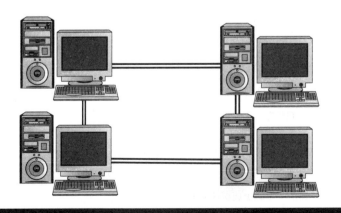

Home Page: It is the first page retrieved when accessing a Web site. It serves as a table of contents to the rest of the pages on the site or to other Web sites. For example, a company's welcome page typically includes the company's logo, a brief description of the company and links to additional documents available on that site.

Hub: All the cables on a network come together at a central location called hub. A hub contains multiple ports.

HTML: HTML are the initials that stand for **H**yper**T**ext **M**arkup **L**anguage. It is a computer language used to create Web pages. Web pages are called HTML documents. HTML documents consist of text and special instructions, called tags. These documents have an html or htm extension, for example: index.html.

Information technology (IT): Any form of technology, ie, any equipment or technique used by people to handle information is called information technology. The information is collected processed, stored and used. Modern information technology combines electronics and telecommunications so that large amounts of data can be stored and transmitted.

Icon: A picture on the screen that represents a specific file, directory or program. By clicking on the icon, you can open the file, directory, window or start a program.

Ink-jet Printer: An ink-jet printer produces high-quality documents at a relatively low price. An ink-jet printer has a print head that sprays ink through small nozzles onto a page. Ink-jet printers usually use individual sheets of paper stored in a removable or stationary tray.

iMac: The iMac is an all-in-one computer that contains components such as a monitor, speakers, hard drive and CD-ROM or DVD-ROM drive in a single unit.

Input Devices: Any hardware component that allows you to enter data, programs, commands and user responses into a computer is an **input device**. Popular input devices include the keyboard, mouse, stylus, microphone, digital camera and scanner.

Insert Key: It is abbreviated as **Ins**. To switch between insert and overwrite mode or to insert an object at the current cursor location, an insert key is used on the keyboard .

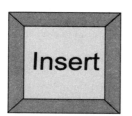

Internet: It is also called the **Net**. It is one of the largest network that links millions or trillions of computers world wide, which are accessible to users via communications devices such as modems, cables, telephone lines and satellites.

Insertion Point: It is a symbol that indicates where a typed character would get displayed on the screen.

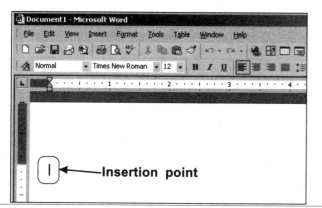

Insertion point

Internet Service Providers (ISP): It is a company that provides access to the Internet for a monthly fee. The service provider gives you a software package, username, password and access phone number.

Internal Modem: It is a type of expansion card that is installed inside the computer and enables a computer to transmit data over telephone or cable lines.

ISDN: It is abbreviated as **I**ntegrated **S**ervices **D**igital **N**etwork, an international communications standard for sending voice, video, and data over digital telephone lines. ISDN supports data transfer rates of 64 Kbps (64,000 bits per second).

JPEG: Shorts for **J**oint **P**hotographic **E**xpert **G**roup. It is a graphical image file that is saved using compression techniques to reduce the file size for downloading it faster from the Web.

Jewel Case: The plastic container used to package an audio CD or CD-ROM disc is called a jewel case.

Jumper: It is a small metal plug that can be connected between different points in an electronic circuit in order to alter an aspect of a hardware configuration. On a hard drive, a jumper selects between master and slave.

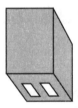

Joystick: It is a long stick attached to a plastic base. It is a lever for controlling the movement of the cursor on the screen of the computer. A joystick usually comes with two control buttons attached to the base or to the stick itself.

Justification: It is the way of printing or displaying text by adjusting the spacing within a document so that lines end evenly at a straight margin.

Kilobit: It is a data unit equal to 1,024 bits. In general usage, it sometimes refers to one thousand bits. It is abbreviated as Kb or kbit.

Key: A key is a button on the keyboard. When a key is pressed, a signal is sent to the computer. Either a character appears on the visual display unit, or a command is carried out.

Kilohertz: It is a unit of frequency equal to 1,000 hertz. It is abbreviated as KHz.

Keyboard: It is a set of typewriter like keys that enables you to enter data into the computer. Desktop computer keyboards typically have 101 to 105 keys.

Kiosk: It is a touch screen computer or terminal that provides information to the public, usually through a multimedia display.

LCD Monitors: LCD is abbreviation of **L**iquid **C**rystal **D**isplay. This type of screen is used on a notebook computer. An LCD monitor uses less electricity, weighs lighter and takes up less desk space but is more expensive than regular monitors.

Laptop: It is a small, lightweight computer that you can easily transport. Laptop computers have the same capabilities as a full-size computer, although laptop computers are more expensive. A laptop computer has a built-in keyboard, pointing device and screen.

Light Pen: A light-sensitive input device is used to select objects on a display screen. A light pen is similar to a mouse, except that with a light pen you can select objects on the display screen by moving the pointer directly on the objects with the pen.

Laser Printer: It is an electrophotographic printer that is based on the technology used by photocopiers. All laser printers can print on $8^{1/2}$ by 11-inch paper, envelopes, labels and transparencies.

Local Area Network (LAN): It is a network that connects computers and devices in a limited geographical area such as home, school computer laboratory, or office building. Each computer or device on the network is a **node** and is connected via cables.

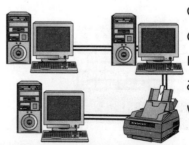

Memory: A computer uses memory to store data and information. The memory chips on the circuit board in the system unit perform this function. A computer contains two types of memory: volatile and nonvolatile. The contents of **volatile memory** are lost when the computer's power is turned off, whereas the contents of **nonvolatile** memory is kept intact in the computer when power is turned off.

Macintosh Computers: Also known as Macs they were introduced by Apple Computer in 1984. Macintosh computers were the first home computers with a mouse, on-screen windows, menus and icons.

Menu Bar: It is a horizontal bar that runs across the top of the screen or a window and contains the names of available menu options.

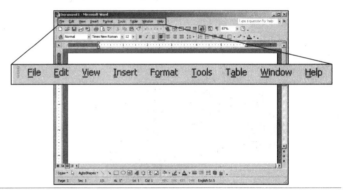

Mainframe: It is a large, expansive, powerful computer that can handle thousands of connected users simultaneously and process upto millions of instructions per second.

Microprocessor: Often called a **processor** which interprets and carries out the basic instructions that operate a computer, it is also called the brain of the computer. Most of the devices connected to the computer communicate with the processor in order to perform a task.

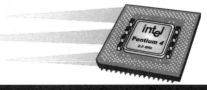

Monochrome: Monochrome means the displaying of information of data in one color (such as white, amber, green, black, blue or gray) against a different colored background, possibly black or grayish-white. Monochrome displays are much cheaper as compared to colored displays.

Monitor: It is an output device which looks like a television screen, and is used to display text or graphics. Monitors for desktop computers are available in various sizes, the most common being 14, 15, 17, 19, 21 and 22 inches.

Modem: Short for **mo**dulator-**dem**odulator, a modem is a device that enables a computer to transmit data over telephone or cable lines. Two types of modems are: Internal modem and external modem.

Mouse: It is an input device that fits comfortably under the palm of your hand. With the help of a mouse, you can control the movement of the mouse pointer on the screen and make selections from the screen. The top of a mouse usually contains one to three buttons.

Motherboard: A large circuit board containing a number of tiny electronic and other components inside the system unit is called a **motherboard.**

Multi-functional Device: A multi-functional printer is a hardware device that combines several functions into one unit; for example, the combination of fax, copier, printer and scanner in one machine. Such devices save money and room on crowded desktops.

Network Card: It is used to provide network access to a computer or other devices, such as a printer. Network interface cards mediate between the computer and the physical media, such as cables, over which transmissions take place.

Netscape Navigator: It is a widely used Web browser program, made by Netscape Corporation. Netscape Navigator, which is based on NCSA's Mosaic Web browser, was one of the first commercially available Web browsers.

Network Operating System: It is a software used to control the overall activity of a network. Network operating systems are powerful programs that are capable of quickly processing large amounts of information.

Network: It is a group of computers and associated devices that are connected by communications facilities. A network can be as small as a LAN (local area network) consisting of a few computers, printers and other devices or it can consist of many small and large computers distributed over a vast geographic area (WAN or wide area network).

Newsgroups: It is discussion group on the Internet. A user sends a message to the newsgroup and other users who read and reply to the message in order to participate in a discussion. An Usenet is the assembly of Internet newsgroups on various topics. Some of the topics are news, recreation, business, science, and computers.

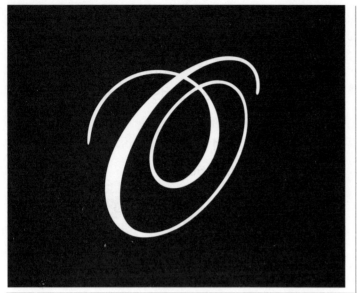

Operating System Software:

This software controls the overall activity of a computer. It is the main program that runs a computer. Most new computers come with the Windows Me or XP operating system software.

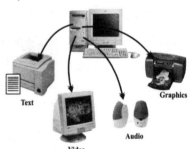

OCR (Optical Character Recognition):

An OCR system enables you to take a book or a magazine article, feed it directly into a computer file with the help of a scanner, and then edit the file using a word processor.

Output Device:

An output device is any hardware component that can convey information to a user. Some commonly used output devices are monitors, printers, speakers, headsets, data projectors, facsimile machines and multi-functional devices.

Text
Graphics
Audio
Video

Online:

Whenever a device is connected to a computer or any telecommunications system, they are referred to online. For example printers are online when they are ready to receive data from the computer. Users are said to be online when they are connected to a computer service through a modem.

Overwrite:

It is a data entry mode that writes over existing characters on screen when new characters are typed in.

Page Down Key: It is a key that moves the cursor down a screenful of lines in most word processing programs.

Packets: These are the small chunks which are broken by the Net while sending the e-mail message from one computer to another. Each packet contains the address of the destination computer. The chunks are put back together to form the e-mail message, when this message reaches the designated computer.

Palmtop: A computer that is small enough to fit in the palm of your hand. These computers may have special keyboard or keypad to enter the data.

Page Break: It is where one page ends and another page starts in a document. It is done automatically in word processing when one page is full.

Passive Matrix: Reading can be difficult in passive matrix screens when viewed from an angle. This type of screen is less expensive than an active matrix screen, and it is not as bright or rich in color.

Password: A sequence of hidden characters that are used to access files and programs in a computer, or network. Many software programs require the user to give a password to a particular file. Only other users who know the password are able to open the file.

Personal Computer (PC): It is a general purpose microcomputer design to be operated by one person at a time. They are used for such purposes as keeping records, writing reports, programming or playing games.

Peer-to-peer Network: It is a network of two or more computers that use the same program or type of program to communicate and share data. All the people on this network store their files on their computers. Anyone on the network can access files stored on any other computer.

Photo Printer: A photo printer is a color printer that can produce photorealistic quality output as well as print everyday documents.

Pen Computer: Any class of computer that lets you input and retrieve data by writing with a special pen instead of keyboard, is called a pen computer.

Printer: An output device that produces a paper copy of the information displayed on the screen is called a **printer**. You can use a printer to produce letters, invoices, and much more. Printed information on paper is called **Hard copy**.

Queue: A queue is a list in a certain order. A printer lists files in a queue. This shows the order in which the original print command for each file was given.

Quicken: It is a popular financial management program for PCs and Macs. It is used to write checks and produce a variety of reports for personal finance and small business.

Query: It is a question you type in a query to request information from a database. For instance, a database of cricket statistics can be queried to mention all the players who scored less than 50 runs in the last 5 games.

QWERTY Keyboard: A standard computer keyboard is sometimes called a QWERTY keyboard because of the arrangement of its keys. That is, the first six leftmost keys on the top alphabetic line of the keyboard spell QWERTY.

Read/write Head: A read-write head is the device used to read and write data. It is a part of a disk drive. The read-write head sends and receives signals between the disk and the computer. The read-write head is very close to the disk when reading data.

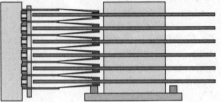

Radio Button: These are a series of on-screen buttons that allow selection of particular tasks. If a button is currently selected, it will get deselected when another button is selected.

Recycle Bin: In Windows 95/98/2000/ME/XP, represented by an icon of a Trash can, it is used for deleting files. The icon of a file or folder is dragged to the trash can and released.

RAM (Random Access Memory): RAM consists of memory chips that can be read from and written by the processor and other devices. When you start your computer, certain operating system files load from a storage device, such as a hard disk, into RAM. These files remain in RAM as long as the computer is running.

Resolution: It is a degree of sharpness of a displayed or printed character or image from the screen. For printers and scanners, resolution is expressed as the number of dots per linear inch. 300 dpi means 300x300, or 90,000 dots per square inch.

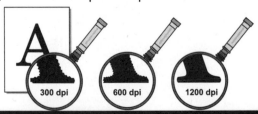

Scroll Lock Key: It is a toggle key that, in some programs, switches the cursor-movement keys between two different modes. The exact function of this key varies among programs.

Scanner: It is a light-sensing input device that reads printed text and graphics and then translates the results into a form the computer can use. Once an object is scanned, it can be displayed on the screen and stored on a storage medium.

Search Engine: A software program or Web site which is used to locate Web sites, Web pages and Internet files is called search engine.

Screen Saver: It is a computer program that usually displays various images on the screen of a computer that is on but not in use so as to prevent damage to the screen's phosphors.

Server: It is a computer that controls and supplies information to connected computers, such as Web servers, mail servers and LAN servers. When a user connects to a server, applications, files, printers and other information and hardware become available.

Shift Key: When the Shift key is pressed in combination with another key it gives that key an alternative meaning; for example, it will produce an uppercase character whenever the shift key is pressed with another alphabet key.

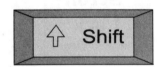

Space Bar: A long bar key at the bottom of the keyboard that, when pressed down, gives a blank space to the right of the typed character on the screen.

Software: It is a set of electronic instructions that control the operation of computer hardware. Operating system and Application are the two types of software. Some popular software are MS Word, MS Excel and MS PowerPoint.

Speakers: It is an output device which allows you to hear the sound generated by your computer. Most computers come equipped with low-quality speakers. You can also purchase high-quality speakers if you want to use your computer to play games or listen to music CDs.

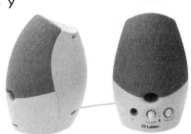

Software Suite: It is a collection of programs sold together in one package.

Storage Devices: Storage devices can be used to store data, instructions and information for future use. Hard drive, floppy disk and compact disc are the main types of storage devices.

Tape Drive: A tape drive reads from and writes data and information on a tape. Although older computers used reel-to-reel tape drives, present day computers use tape cartridges. PC users sometimes keep a backup of hard disks on tapes.

Tab Key: To move the cursor to a preset distance, as to the next cell in a spreadsheet or to another part of a dialog box, the tab key is used.

Text: Text is information, or data, in the form of words and numbers typed in a computer. Text is input using a keyboard or a scanner. A wordprocessor is often used to work with text on a computer.

Tags: In languages like HTML, a code that identifies an element in a document, such as a heading or a paragraph, for the purpose of formatting, indexing, and linking information in the document, tags are used. Angle brackets < > are used for enclosing each HTML tag giving a specific instruction. Most tags have an opening tag and a closing tag that affect the text between the tags.

Token Ring: When all the computers are arranged (schematically) in a circle, it is known as a token-ring network. A token, which is a special bit pattern, travels around the circle. Message is passed from one computer to next until it reaches its destination.

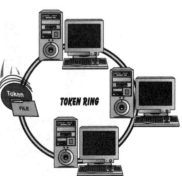

Toner: Laser printers use a fine powdered ink, called toner, which comes in a cartridge, like photocopiers.

Trackball: It is a pointing device with a ball on its top. To move the pointer using a trackball, you rotate the ball with your thumb, fingers or the palm of your hand. In addition to the ball, a trackball usually has one or more buttons that work just like mouse buttons.

Touchpad: It is a small, rectangular pointing device that is sensitive to pressure and motion. To move the pointer using a touchpad, you slide your fingertip across the surface of the pad. Some touchpads have one or more buttons around the edge of the pad that work like mouse buttons.

Touchpad

Twisted Pair Cable: It contains one or more pairs of copper wires. The copper wires in each pair are twisted around each other. By twisting the wires around each other, the cable is less prone to interference from other electrical signals, such as the signals emitted by photocopiers or alarm systems.

Tower Case: A tower case has a tall and narrow system unit. It usually sits on the floor vertically. Tower cases come in different sizes.

Typeface: The design of a set of printed characters, such as Courier, Helvetica and Times New Roman.

Universal Serial Bus (USB): It is a hardware interface for low-speed peripherals such as the keyboard, mouse, joystick, scanner and printer. Peripherals can be plugged in and unplugged without turning the system off.

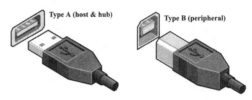

Type A (host & hub)   Type B (peripheral)

Uniform Resource Locator (URL): It is the address that defines the route to a file on the Web. URLs are typed into the browser to access Web pages. The URL contains the protocol prefix, domain name, subdirectory names and file name. For example:

Http://www.sterlingpublishers.com

Uninterruptible Power Supply (UPS): A power supply containing a battery source that supplies power to the computer in case the main supply fails.

Video conferencing: It allows three or more participants to sit in a conference room and communicate with each other online. Each participant has a video camera, microphone, and speakers mounted on his or her computer.

Virtual Reality: Virtual reality is a way of creating a three-dimensional image of an object or scene. It makes it possible for the user to move through or around the image.

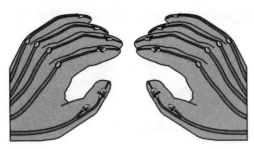

Virus: A virus can badly affect or infect your computer system without your knowledge and alter the functions of your computer. Once a virus is in your computer, your files and operating system may be damaged. A virus can severely damage your files and operating system.

Web browser: A Web browser, or browser, is a software program that allows you to access and view Web pages. Web browser software is built on the concept of **hyperlinks**, which allows users to point and click with a mouse in order to jump from document to document in whatever order they desire. Web browsers are of two kinds: text-only browsers and graphical Web browsers.

Volatile memory: It is the type of memory whose contents are lost (erased) when the computer's power is turned off. RAM (random access memory) is an example of volatile memory.

Web page: It is a electronic document on the World Wide Web. A vast amount of information is provided by these Web pages. The information may include graphics, sound or even movies. A Web page usually contains links to other Web pages.

Web site: It is a collection of Web pages. Most Web sites have a home page as their starting point, which frequently functions as a table of contents for the site. Users need a Web browser and an Internet connection to access a Web site.

Windows: It is an operating system introduced by Microsoft Corporation in 1983. Windows is a multitasking graphical user interface environment.

X-axis: It is the horizontal axis in a two-dimensional graph or coordinate system.

World Wide Web (WWW): It is a way of accessing and presenting information in a multimedia-rich form. Graphics, sound, video, animation and formatted text can all be made available via the 'Web'. The information is presented on a page at a time and each page contains highlighted links — called hyperlinks and these links could be words, pictures, or graphics.

XML: Abbreviation of EXtensible Markup Language. A document format for the Web that is more flexible than HTML. While HTML uses only predefined tags to describe elements within the page, XML allows tags to be defined by the developer of the page. XML is a subset of the SGML document language, and HTML is a document type of SGML.

ZIF Socket: It also called **Z**ero **I**nsertion **F**orce socket. It is a type of socket designed for easy removing and replacing of CPU chips for upgrading the computer. The chip is dropped into the socket's holes and a lever is pulled down to lock it in.

Yahoo!: Launched in 1994, it is trademark for an Internet search engine based on the World Wide Web. Yahoo is the Web's oldest 'directory', a place where human editors organize web sites into categories. www.yahoo.com

Zip Disk: A trademark for a removable hard disk technology developed by Iomega Corporation that can store up to 100MB of data.

Zoom: This feature is used to enlarge a selected portion of a image or document to fill a window or the screen. Zooming is a feature that allows the user to select a small part of the image, zoom it, and make changes to the enlarged portion at a finer level of detail.